The Impossible Physics of the Hummingbird

by Kim Farrar

Attention schools and businesses: for discounted copies on large
orders, please contact the publisher directly.

For information contact:
Unsolicited Press
Portland, Oregon
www.unsolicitedpress.com
orders@unsolicitedpress.com
619-354-8005

Cover Design: Kathryn Gerhardt
Editor: Summer Stewart
ISBN: 978-1-963115-51-2

to Rob

Were it not for the way you taught me to look
at the world, to see the life at play in everything,
 I would have to be lonely forever.

Ted Kooser

TABLE OF CONTENTS

The Impossible Physics of the Hummingbird

I.

Nature

SPIDER

Down the soft log steps,
around the bend we run
into the Kentucky woods.
You stoop, I stoop.

Look there, you instruct,
a perfect spider's web.
Each glistening fiber
jeweled with dew.

The first Dream Catcher,
at its center she rests,
each leg a gorgeous black hair
tapered to a pin's point.

Red speckles across her abdomen,
we guess she's pregnant and venomous.
You teach me about creatures—
bright colors fatally tempt predators.

You flip a toupee of sod and twigs
to investigate what's underneath.
A grub, so ugly and pale, in her presence
but you swear they make the best bait.

We eventually return. Forty years later,
I cannot write your eulogy when she re-appears
with her spinnerets to offer me a thread,
says: Begin with this story.

CONVERSATIONS WITH MY BROTHER

Last night on Jeopardy, I learned the octopus
classifies as phylum Mollusca, thanks to tentacles
originated from the mollusk foot 500 million years ago.
Our favorite—the Cambrian Era.

When I shared my factoid with my husband,
he replied, *Uh-huh, that's interesting*,
but my brother and I roamed the land
of giant trilobites and swimming millipedes.

Together we'd enter the realm of the curious,
but now I'm stuck with half a conversation
deferred, no one to confirm the bat colonies
in my mind, the dinosaurs becoming birds.

CALAMITIES OF THE NATURAL WORLD

Few things frighten me more
than a *New York Times* interactive graphic,
the nerve-wracking data amassing
as trends arc toward certain catastrophe.

Fact: the crack in the Antarctic shelf
lengthened seventeen miles in just two months.
The red line slithers around Larsen C,
the huge puzzle piece about to dislodge.

Larsen A and B have already calved
into the ocean without much hoopla,
but Larsen C supports two ice anchors
against complete collapse.

It makes me miss my brother.
Our conversations often swirled
around calamities of the natural world.
I want to call him

and ask, *What's up with the Antarctic shelf?*
He'd know the story, being up to date
on Smithsonian and National Geographic,
but perhaps behind on car payments.

He'd tell me that Larsen C isn't the worry;
it's the bergs exposed as their giant ice tutu
drifts south. We'd talk about the neglect,
the steady but deadly erosion.

Some disasters are so long in the making.
 Our topics let us discuss destruction,
the sadness of extinction: things done,
unchangeable losses.

My brother with no proper bedding
and one dinner plate, but I tried not to judge.
You had to love him whole, you had to
love his whole slow falling apart.

TELESCOPE STILTS

you will go on telescope stilts
far away into the certain darkness
   —Zbigniew Herbert

I finally grasped the ghostly nature of stars
whose light can travel long after their cores collapse.

I turned our telescopes to the ground.
The universe, such a disappointment, mostly empty space.

I needed some height, some perspective,
so I re-fashioned our brass companions as stilts.

Satisfaction in the twist and click, as each cylinder
locked into place for the last time.

 It was good—the small problems to solve.

The lens caps became rubber skids. Old switch-plates
were strapped to the focus knobs as footholds.

I felt better on my stilts, lifting each foot
with its heavy weight, learning to balance.

My center of gravity was off-kilter, pivoting
left and right, forward and back.

I learned to scissor-step with some grace.

I ventured out again,
above the clamor and the demanding eye-contact.

Even our mother understood.
How could I walk around like you were alive?

DEAR PLUTO

If any planet had possibilities, it was you
with your wobbly, erratic orbit. An outsider,
but still in. Why did we abandon you
to spin on the brim of our solar system?
Outcast among the riffraff pulled by gravity
and dark matter, now nobody's son.
They tell us you're a dime-a-dozen ice ball
that should never have been given the high status of planet.
I understand their point: if *you're* a planet
then we have to accept every dork, every lopsided meteor,
the uncharted, the borderline cases. The neat elliptical paths
of our exclusive cosmic neighborhood
morphing into a chaotic web.
Science demands elegance, but you gave me hope
that even the glum and unspectacular
might join the club. I worry about you, orphaned
and shunned, taking your slow 248 years
to orbit the sun, shuffled onto the Kuiper Belt
with its masses of asteroids and space junk.
Already disappeared from texts and diagrams,
who will cherish you? Who will remember?

24

ORBITS AND BONDS

You explained the atomic world with its orbits
and bonds, as we counted Mississippis
between lightning bolt and thunderclap:

The booms were super-heated molecules
crashing back together after the zap.
You stung me with a rubber band as proof.

*

Why was that ladder open in your living room?
Did you plan to fix a distant light,
or sweep a silverfish from the ceiling?

The apartment was a surrealist still life
with two empty fish tanks and a village
of dead electronics in the corner.

Three fishing poles still in their shipping tubes
were under the bed, each ordered at 3 am,
as you began to dream of a quieter place.

You meant to be a naturalist with a safari vest
but mostly drove a cement truck, one elbow
out the window, a pack of Marlboro reds on the dash.

*

Today a green strip of algae is trapped
in the washer's portal and I wonder if hot
or cold is best to prevent infiltration.

I ponder the miracle of algae:
the first photosynthesis, the first food,
the first oxygenating organism.

The primordial soup bubbled hot
and you called that mix *algae heaven*,
so I turn the dial to cold and get on with it.

PANDEMIC DAWN

Outside my window the sky is reliable:
a bank of grey-pink clouds recedes,
heading back to Coney Island.

The yellow brick facade
across the avenue is Deco influenced,
the cornice etched by age and weather.

A little ruin is a comfort.
The sunlight slices the building top
and I ponder the high angle, the unrisen sun.

A pair of pigeons lifts my gaze to the rooftop
where a metal unit bears graffiti
that looks Germanic, umlaut and everything:

Fräf Ger 357
Mr. E

And momentarily I have a little faith
in crazy human ingenuity. How
did Mr. E get up there and do that?

Gennero's Salumeria boarded up
is a reminder of the sorrow
I want to keep out of this poem.

The sun ignites the facade a blinding,
Byzantine gold and a couple strolls by
kissing through blue surgical masks.

TO THE MONK PARROTS OF ASTORIA

Little green gossips, tell me,
—long-tailed, snappy dressers—
how do you like New York?

Your chatter and surprise
welcome during the Covid quiet.

How many years will I repeat
There go the parrots
every time you wheel overhead?

On a lockdown walk
a neighbor sees me searching.
They're in my apple tree, he yells
from the porch. *They eat all my apples.*
I don't care. I let them live there.
I thrill at his unplaceable accent,
tear up over simple kindness.

Tell me, parrots:
Do you miss the wild seeds in South America?
Are you homesick or too busy surviving?

Classified now as *accidentals* or *exotics*
like most of us non-Indigenous
that land in this city.

You have saved me more than once,
the squawks without rainforest
reminding me of what's possible.

Tell me how to be brighter?

If your flock grows to a hundred,
we call it a Company of Parrots.

AUTONOMY, 1967

Whispering to a cardinal
outside the kitchen window
that he's a handsome boy
is how I want to remember her,
      not parked in a hallway
      with her tee shirt a mess
      of old stains and lunch crumbs
      which no one seems to notice.
I didn't sneak behind her that day long ago,
she was absorbed and this shut me up
from asking what there was to eat
or if she'd seen my shoes anywhere.
      My mother's shoes disappear
      from the nursing home. I took back
      her porcelain bear and glass whale
      before they were pilfered
      from her *Memory Shelf.*
I couldn't hear the wish she made
that day as she stood in her birthright
to be left alone to talk to birds.
      I want to freeze-frame that woman
      before she turned
and asked what I was looking for.

THE OLD CAT

She's an old scrap of a cat,
but she used to be a hunter.
Silent and focused, she could
hear a cockroach inside a wall.

Now she yawls at 3am,
as globs of food drop
from her misaligned jaw,
her bowl is a crusty mess.
Someday we all become
bad dinner guests.

She was once luxurious, soft
and preened, not matted and patchy.
Half the time I think she's dead
or a dusty sock tossed on the bed.

She sleeps, sleeps, sleeps.
I will miss her heat in the bed,
so I debate when to kill her.
How much longer can she drag
her rear end down the hall?

There was a time she could spring
to the top of my dresser— back arched,
legs relaxed. She'd land without a sound
and smirk in my direction.

I can't find the time
to make the appointment.
She was a fine animal,
my aloof companion.

When will I sleep, sleep, sleep,
bored by the wait
for no more heartbeats?

ODE TO THE TURTLE

Old diligence, basking
on your enduring flagstone
of self-reliance.
You are a mound
of patience. Your eyes
masked by a yellow
racing stripe, a touch
of slick irony.

You are a testament
to the advantage
of closing up.
Where is the giant sloth
with his great hooked claws?
Or, the saber-toothed
tiger with his over-sized fangs?
Such audacity—
unlearned in the art
of withdrawal.

If evolution is change,
you are the mascot
for sticking with what works.
The permanent frown

and calloused beak
deny the bean-sized heart
protected between
plastron and carapace.

Your walk tetters
like a ship tossed at sea—
loose cargo shifting
in the hold—suffering
the weight of carrying
one's home everywhere.

MEDITATION ON GEORGE THE SNAIL, THE LAST OF HIS SPECIES

The snail is my mascot.
Moving slowly is my forte.
Making the slightest progress
is a way to keep going, right George?
You were one of the first things I could draw.

I'm sorry to admit it but, as a kid,
I tortured your cousin, the slug, in a jar
with salt. I observed his membranes dry,
his body wither like a raisin.
After several days, I unscrewed the lid
and shook him half-dead back into the garden,
as if that saved either of us from my sin.

Tonight, my mother says, *I can't walk
like I want to*, her back hunched,
legs shining like plastic, we move
down the walkway, taking the tiniest steps,
a snail's pace. I practice going slower
than my slowest. When she passes,
she will be the last of ten siblings.

We spent a day at Winton Woods
watching the ducks and paddleboats,
not saying much. Our silence comfortable,
not yet a sign of her being lost.

George, I'll be still now.
Linger with me awhile.
I take my time, George,
because good-bye is never far.

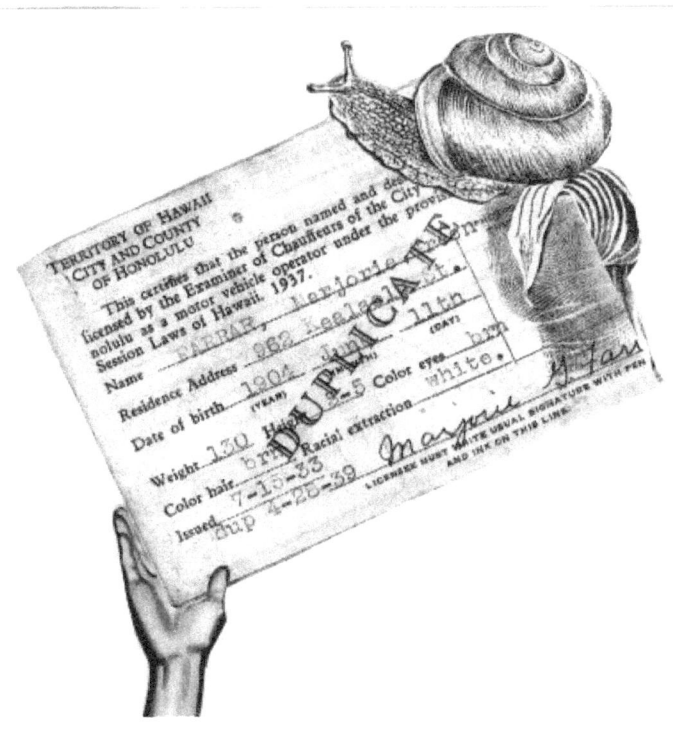

ANOTHER OLD CAT

He still loves food. Hunger–
that primary drive moves him
to lap gelatin from his turkey bits
to his toothless gums.
No chewing necessary,
old-cat applesauce.

I hope when it's my applesauce time,
eyes clouded, teeth gone,
that someone will stand nearby,
and watch me with equal affection.

Powerful Forces

Watching my autistic daughter stand at the ocean's edge,
I imagine that words for her are sound clusters in primary colors.

But today, I forget about trying to extract language,
trying to hear her voice. The ocean fills the space
where the trying goes.

Such powerful forces—light, motion, moon-pull—
are no match for her stillness.

I stand far enough behind to resist reaching for her elbow.

She listens to the rhythms, absorbs the mist through her skin
as each wave reaches critical momentum, curling into itself.

All day we hallucinate dolphins in the ocean's shimmy.

The horizon makes me feel like I'm a ghost in her future.

The sky is layered with shaded greys,
yet the entire scene glows,
my daughter's hair so gold, all I can think is—

Lord, look how beautiful she is. Lord,
let others love how she lifts her face to the wind.

WHEN

We have a picture of her
When clouds were calligraphy
and her grandmothers sent forbidden candies
When my wedding dress waited inside her hope chest
and the rabbit curled with her sisters in the den
When honeybees were common
and the apple tree was green and unsplit
Before the lightning turned its bark to tar
and the honeybees disappeared
Before the rabbit's anguished cry in the cat's jaws
Before the wedding dress was boxed and donated
and her grandmothers sent prayers
Before every cloud threatened flood
We have a picture of her
when we still believed it was Eden

THE SCHOLAR'S COURTYARD AT THE METROPOLITAN MUSEUM OF ART

We step through the moon gate and the light
brightens after the dim halls of art. We breathe
deeply; here your silence is reverie,
everywhere else it's autism.

Lattice motifs lace the courtyard.
Symmetry and pattern, even the shadows
are woven. A grey stone riddled by ancient rains
balances like Buddha beneath two round windows.

It's as if the gods themselves drew
these garden blueprints: A shorn juniper,
shaped by hand not hurricane, yet windswept
after years of training. We listen.

Water trickles down the miniature cliffs
into the pool, where we wait patiently
for the lazy koi. A sign warns us
against wishing: Please, no coins.

II.
Lessons

WALKING TO LaGUARDIA COMMUNITY COLLEGE

There's a kooky intersection
on Thompson Avenue
where students and faculty,
staff and security,
converge from slanted side streets.
Each of us lost
in our private thoughts,
rehearsing the day ahead.

A sudden wind blew us messy,
whipped my hair into a frenzy,
everyone loosened,
laughed more readily.
A young woman
just behind the line
of my peripheral vision
said, *There's a leaf in your hair,*
gently plucked it from my nest.
The rhythm echoed from childhood:
and also with you…

I turned and
her beauty stunned—

large amber eyes,
radiant black skin,
her sweet voice
as she whispered,
Maybe it's good luck,
and why not?
No speck
or notch on its golden,
waxy surface—
good luck to touch
as she placed the leaf
in my palm before
the light changed,
the traffic stopped,
and we all crossed
in orchestra.

SHE-MONSTER GETS FIRED

Here you go again, running from the villagers
with their torches and pitchforks.
You thought you finally fit in.
You filed down your neck-bolts,
got rid of your high-waters.

You watched Oprah, kept a dream diary,
a gratitude journal, pictures of your thinner self
on the fridge. You tried to keep your need
for electricity minimized: licking the outlets,
rubbing your hair with a balloon for just a crackle.

It took years of practicing the right laugh.
You did your best. Married up.
Got a job teaching ESL. Now and then,
a grunt would slip and

crickets   crickets   crickets.

Every morning, the affirmations,
the meditation, the positive thinking.
You longed for lightning and rain.
You did everything right to escape
the old ways of staring into the well.

People liked you. You were funny.
But one day you got caught
eating flies in the faculty lounge
and soon the rumors started.

You missed being the girl
who loved her square head,
touched her thick-stitched scars like Braille—
so you stopped hiding your green
undertones with foundation.

The villagers yell, *Kill her!*
Kill the monster! You barrel
through the woods, nettles whip
your ankles as you soar over logs
in your clodhoppers. You're filled
with the old familiar joy of being
outcast and incredible.

BEFUDDLED

I don't speak Cantonese
or Mandarin, and she spoke
little English, yet kindly
explained each scroll
adorning the stairwell
inside Chung Hwa Bookshop
in Flushing, New York.

This one happiness. This fortune.
This family. Then she paused,
slightly panicked, and rushed
to her register for a stashed index card.
The creases were soft as fur
from many unfoldings, and printed
there in all-caps was BEFUDDLED.

This one befuddled
and our heads cocked in doubt.
Did she mean it befuddled her
or the scroll signified befuddlement?
How had that peculiar word
landed here? What seas had it crossed,
what deserts, to be inked on a card
in the palm of her hand?

Perhaps she copied it
from a battered phrase book,
or when she asked a bilingual friend,
he said, *I'm befuddled,*
and she had him spell it out.

The scroll had six prawns—
four paddling in one direction,
with two turning left.
Maybe it meant befuddled after all,
but it easily could have been
knowledge or *friendship* or *destiny*
as we searched each other's eyes
for understanding. Then, in the clarity
of our human need, I said: *I'll take it.*

THE GIFT

The crystal forget-me-nots
shipped to my mother
at Seasons Senior Living
cost 31 cents after rewards points.

I worried the trinket might fling
from her tray that swivels
in the narrow lane
between wheelchair and bed.

The space used to brace
the harness and crane
that lift her as the cable
cranks around the winch.

But maybe an aide
would gently cup my gift,
situate it on the sill,
for safekeeping, care enough

to calculate the limits
of her vision when she scans
the room for some familiar hint—
Where are my paisley curtains?

And maybe sunlight would glint
off my glass flowers like a mirror
signaling a rescue-copter and she'd feel,
I don't know, more like a woman loved.

The tracking updates excited me. *It's in Florida.*
Now, Missouri, Ma. A blizzard delayed
anticipated dates, the location providing
a ready-made topic for our brief calls.

The gift was delivered but never arrived,
misplaced inside the complex. For weeks,
I surmised the trinket's whereabouts,
made cheerful promises about tomorrow.

I'm often put through
to the same wrong mom
who tells me her sleeping pills
are red and smell funny.

It almost doesn't matter
she isn't my mother, I'm not
her daughter, I listen
with the same impotence.

My mother tells me to quit
talking about those flowers
and I do, finally, surrender.

To Jon Anderson

1940-2007

I pull book after book from the shelf
as I search for *In Sepia*, your book.
My eyes strain from distractions:
Roethke's *Elegy for Jane*, the index in Turco,
and, of course, Bogan's *Blue Estuaries*
spill across the table. Are you impressed, Jon?
I want to show how much I've learned
since you patted my first poem on your desk.
When you exhaled your wife's name...Barbara...
I always thought of a globe.

I appreciated the way your hands shook
as you lifted that paper coffee cup
to your mustachioed lip. It was good to be scared
with you in Poetry 101. A few times since then
I have imagined us staring out our windows
at the same moment. That first verse scrawled
and mimeographed in purple ink, very dramatic,
something about globs of goo in feeding tubes.
You gave it back to me, holding the paper
with two hands as if it were a sacred parchment.
I can't recall a single lecture, or any words of wisdom,

but a quietness as you laid down one stone and said,
Step here, it's safe,

then placed another
and taught me to follow after the poem.

ETYMOLOGY

Today I used the word *pentimento*,
stored since 1973, when Lillian Hellman's
bestseller of the same title was the rage.
My friend explained in her flower-power
bedroom what pentimento meant.
I was amazed by two things: First,
that a pencil trace can reappear
from beneath layers of thick paint.
Second, that it sounded like pimento.
I tucked that word away, one sock
inside another. Today, with the heavy fog,
I used it to describe the trees through mist.
I resurrected that word from beneath
50 years of living. A shadow emerged
of two young girls sitting on a bed
to plan their fame and fortune.

To My Old Lewis Turco *The Book of Forms*

I fell for your strange lace
of unstressed *X*'s, the beautiful
a bb a cc patterns, mysterious codes
I didn't grasp, but liked the look of.
The primitive language of rhythm:
bada bada da bum dada.

I wish you were my honeybun,
a favorite example
of pronominal elision
resting between ink stars.
My coffee stains, wine rings,
mark but don't mar.
We understood each other:
you put up with my poor memory,
I tolerated a bit of arrogance.
My highlights faded
into your browning pages,
your paper soft
as a powdered cheek.
A slender book, easy
to hold in one hand
while conducting the air—

but I feared my aging,
and finally threw you away,
excited to welcome the new
revised edition—a black Cadillac,
expanded and updated,
twice as fat.

This new binding resists
and when I look up *Petrarchan*,
my gaze doesn't wander
the way I once strayed
over your curious pages.
I don't use this one much.
Every time I open it,
I am a stranger.

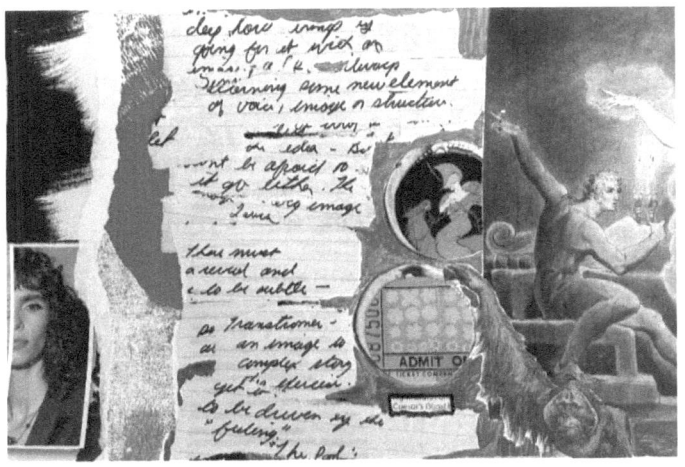

ODE TO A DUMPSTER

Seventeen years I stared out my window at you,
so like any other dumpster. A battle-worn ship,
scraped and scuffed, your lid flipped open,
revealing a huge cube of emptiness.

The ruckus you made being pushed
into your parking place. One wheel roped on,
you wobbled miserably. I'm tired of the young.

All those days I accomplished nothing, you remained
doubtless: There would be waste. I especially liked
the cabbage heads dumped in by the bodega worker,
the soft plop of the unselected.

You withstood the graffiti, the slander.
A fake Latin Kings crown scribbled by local
Greek kids. The heart with 4-ever sprayed inside.
You were there when my father died. It rained sardines.

My new view is a sycamore complete with seed balls
and perky spring leaves, but you, my squat and heavy comrade,
said: *I'm just an old dumpster. Don't mind me.*
I loved you for that.

Remember the cat carcass I could never work into a poem?
The tree nods, but what does she know
of life's drudgery? Always blooming and fading,
whispering: *Change, grow, be natural.*

I miss your old crates, plastic bags, rotten tomatoes
while I toiled to make art from air, filling the trashcan
with mint wrappers, butts, crumpled pages. I miss you
who never once demanded a metaphor.

CONSTRUCTION SITE

Heaps of manmade parts—coils, blocks, stuff—
What to call those giant mandibles? Those iron gizmos?
Contemplating this assorted mess, I realize
I have no vocabulary.

Unable to name what I observe, I panic.
Some say, *Without language, there is no experience*—
a concept I grapple with daily, being both logophile
and mother to my non-verbal autistic daughter.

I am illiterate in pink, spray-painted codes.
What are those concrete rings?
What is that mound of special dirt for?
Those rolls of wire mesh have a name.

The workers, blueprints in hand,
happily navigate between puddles.
They have a clear plan, steps to follow.
I have my desperation for her to one day ask,
What is that, Mom? so I can answer, *I don't know.*

WE COUNT TO THREE

My daughter has been crowing for thirteen years,
then asking, *What does a rooster say?*
Some days her charms are irresistible,

and I *cock-a-doodle-do* like a mate
lost in a cornfield. This is wrong
according to <u>Overcoming Autism</u>.

I should redirect the conversation
to something in front of us,
make her touch the carpet and say, *soft.*

When she was born, her father
held her up and her mouth made
a perfect O, as if we had some nerve,

pulling her from that dark warmth
into fluorescent light. She scored
well on the Apgar, and without knowing,

I rejoiced in her future
all she would learn, every cloud
I could show her, who she might become.

In the park where she played
a stone frog spouted a water arc,
but rather than dart and giggle

with the other little girls
in their ruffled bottoms,
she'd squat by the drain and listen

to the dripping echo in the deep,
metallic well. Now, she's a good swimmer,
and at the pool she 'blends',

until an honest boy asks, *What's wrong with her?*
I explain as best I can. He disappears among the swarms
of screaming children. We count to three and go under.

How to Talk to an Autistic Child

First, be still. Sit within her orbit.
Observe the way she leans into her floppy run.

Wait.

The autistic child looks down, but sees
every glimmer in the sidewalk,
every blonde hair on your arm.

Do something physical and silent.
Make a surprised face, open your mouth
and widen your eyes.

You could nod your head or dance
a little, spin slowly.
When she looks at you,
do it again.

You could try blowing
in your soda bottle to make
a deep jug sound.

Sit on the floor and gently toss a pillow.
Whisper something simple

like, *Fun* or *Oh, boy.*
She may repeat what you say or stop.

When she runs away,
let her.

DIRECTIONS

1.) When you land at the Cincinnati Airport you're really in northern Kentucky.

2.) You must answer "Bengals" when the man in the Avis exit booth asks, "Bengals or Browns?" Otherwise, he might delay for a good thirty seconds pushing the button that raises the traffic arm. Take a right.

3.) Follow the signs for I-275 to I-75. You will have to drive about thirty minutes until you cross the Ohio River on a double-decker, rusted bridge that has a name no one uses. It's just The Bridge as opposed to The Yellow Bridge or The-Bridge-that-Goes-to-Newport.

4.) Just before launching onto the artery that feeds The Bridge there is a long, swooping bend known in local folklore as Deadman's Curve. The warning sign shows a box truck speeding downhill with its back wheels bucking. On the narrow shoulder any blown rubber tread or glittering safety glass is ominous, both past and future. I never knew anyone who wrecked on that curve but right out of high school a drunk driver killed Benny three minutes away from his new apartment.

5.) You will come around Deadman's Curve like a sling shot and straight ahead erupts the Cincinnati skyline. You can't type 'Skyline' without thinking 'Skyline Chili', also known as Cincinnati Chili, that glistening, no-grade beef floating in an oily cinnamony sauce. It's nasty. But, it can seem like a good idea at a buzzed two o'clock in the morning. Whenever I tell someone in New York that I'm originally from Cincinnati, they'll mention Skyline Chili. I remain silent, conflicted between my hometown's ignoble claim to fame and loyalty.

6.) Follow the signs for 71 North. 71 and 75 split at the end of The Bridge. Stay in the two right lanes because the two left lanes head toward Dayton. That way you'll drive past a massive plaster Jesus with outstretched arms and a billboard of a woman kneeling with shackled wrists that proclaims you are hell bound for your lustful ways. The pornographic and violent picture makes one think. Two seconds before, bondage had been the last thing on your mind. You may have been watching the blinking red light atop the Eiffel Tower at Kings Island amusement park and wondering why replicas are depressing. So, stay true to the two right lanes.

7.) Go past The Great American Ball Park that was paid for after a few years voting against the school levy and for the new stadium. The Reds and the Bengals—creating family bonds that survive abuse, neglect, cruelty, betrayal, alcoholism, incest, and secrecy. Go, Bengals!

8.) Go through the tunnel and when you come out the other end, on the left there will be an immediate drop in per-capita income. You will see corroded apartment buildings and mostly African-Americans. On the right, the Natural History Museum sits perched on a high hill. (Inside is a wonderous faux cave complete with blind, albino fish.) Behind that is Mt. Adams, a once destitute Appalachian slum. The stilted houses were slipping down the hillside into the river, but now they are million-dollar town homes with original details. Boutiques selling handcrafted stash boxes from Indonesia long ago replaced the shops with crusted cheeses and bargain candies. The tall thin houses offer a lot of vertical distance between the basement where kids can screw and the third floor where parents chain smoke.

9.) Once under the rusting M.L.K. pedestrian bridge, the next exits are Smith-Edwards Road, Dana Avenue, Kennedy, and finally, you hit the Montgomery Road. Take a left at the end of the ramp. Across from the light is a dilapidated Quality Inn that used to have a seafood restaurant called Dockside. The fried shrimp smell did not wash out of the polyester sailor uniforms and the buffet table was laden with chicken livers. Your hungover waitress was likely nauseous and overheated.

10.) Take a right on Montgomery. Go past the dive bar where the windows are blacked-out with tar paper. (It's open on Thanksgiving when you may need to process your mother's tips on how to grow out your Astor Barber buzz cut.) Go past the gun shop, the florist, and take another right on Indian Mound. The road is gashed with potholes. When the Ford factory closed twenty-seven years ago, they took their tax base with them. In some Faustian political bargain, Norwood is still ineligible for city road repair dollars. But never fear, it's passable.

11.) Take a left on Parmalee at the top of the mound where two beautifully patinated water towers, sea-foam green, stand sentry behind a church that looks like a regular house.

12.) Take a quick right on Wakefield Place. Park your car. You have arrived at my mother's house. Take a few deep breaths to remind yourself that you're happy with the choices you've made because she will begin by asking, "When are you coming home?"

III.
EVOLUTION

RED GRAFFITI

I am older now
in the fenced playground
where the same name or a near birthday
was cause for best-friendship.

Both of us married, in our removed
houses, no longer a simple
walk across Lenox Place
to share a cigarette
stashed in my sock.

The Ohio River snakes fast and black
beyond the underpass where we
once found a fortress
of broken glass and red graffiti.
I come here to be there
with one struck match,
facing the reckless wind.

SYNESTHESIA

the rain falls
in improvised beats
bigger drops plop
through finer mist
and when I sketch
the rain, the paper
becomes a drum
of player piano music

ICE

I like the molecular shutdown
of those frenzied atoms
stacking themselves
into organized bunks.

I like the thick ice
that fractures
but doesn't break.

I appreciate its warning:
Pay attention here.
Beware on the bridge.

There is a German Shepherd
frozen in the reservoir.
Ice preserves.

I like the polar caps
that hold the cracked
egg of Earth.

THE BRASS TAG

Not even my brother's name
is stamped on the thin brass tag
that IDed his sack of ashes.

Greater Cincinnati Crematory
Cremation Number
12203

No one accompanied him
when he burned. The director
warned us that it was all
pretty industrial.

A hole is punched
in one bent corner
for threading it onto a cord.
Who twists the bags
and ties them off?
I should've known more,
asked more questions.

After the scattering,
my sister slipped the tag
into my palm, whispered,

You can use this
in one of your wacky collages.

I keep it in a rusted Altoids tin
along with wildflower seeds
from Dad's service and the collar
of my dead cat, Simon.

Inside my little grave box
there's also a stone given
by a street-fair Hari Krishna.

I thought my brother might like it—
the way it's misty like the quartz
we prized and hunted
in the backyard gravel pile
that never turned into a patio.

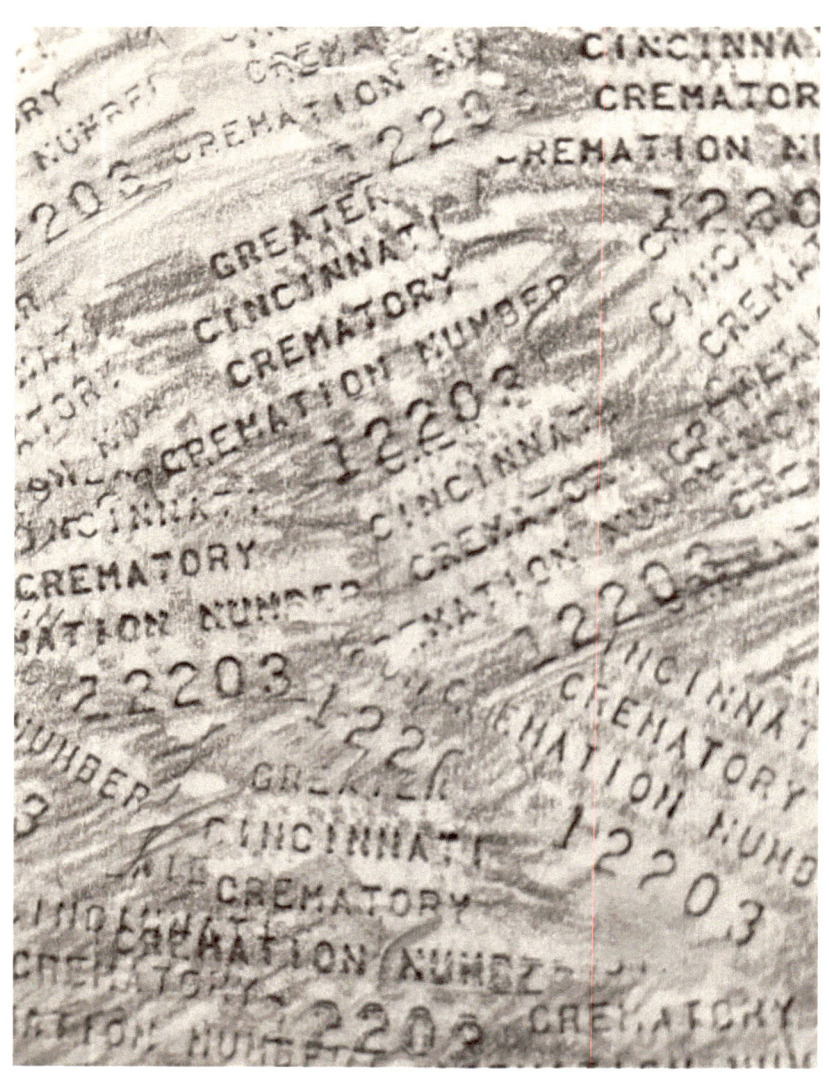

WHY IT'S HARD TO WRITE ABOUT MY BROTHER

Because Rob called me Numbnut,
      and now no one does.
Because in therapy I learned the word *infantilize,*
      and stopped asking if he was alright.
Because I'd rather recite his favorite paperbacks
      as a requiem: Dune, Slaughterhouse-Five, Silent Spring.
Because he taught me how to give the finger when I was six
        and ran when I taught mom.
Because I listened outside the bathroom as he cursed
      Dad for buzz-cutting his curly hair.
Because he comforted my worry that his tetras were bored,
      They have no memory, Numbnut,
      each swim across the tank is a new ocean
      and then I envied their easy forgetting.
Because his longest relationship
      was with a club-footed lovebird he adored.
Because he said I couldn't get good at Sudoku,
      so he could beat me at something.
Because he could pinch open the beak of a baby robin
      to feed it drops of milk.
Because he once touched me and I let him.
Because driving drunk and wrecking cars
      was a form of apology for being a disappointing son.

Because I'd question the impossible physics of the hummingbird,
       to spin the conversation away from his troubles.
Because at fifty-four he could still bruise the same spot
       with a quick knuckle-punch to the arm.
Because we discussed the etymology of kerfuffle
       but never mentioned emphysema.
Because the last time he lit a Marlboro to rest,
       I bummed one and joined him.
Because they zipped him into a midnight body bag
       and left without sirens.
Because he drove me around the city with the windows down
       to point at all the cement he'd poured—
       the post office flagpole, Kroger's sidewalk—
       what he liked about the job
       was leaving something permanent.
Because our last day together was at the aquarium
       watching the sharks swim overhead,
       nets of light reflecting on their underbellies.
Because he'd withdraw for months,
       but I left him messages anyway
because he loved my dream of him.

I BRING PANERA FRUIT SALAD TO MY MOTHER AT THE HOME

The napkin is folded thin like an accordion fan to easily slip into the plastic sleeve with the doll-sized salt and pepper packets and utensils. Mom slides the napkin onto her bed-tray, lifts it and begins unfolding. She smooths each crease against the flat tray, brushes her palms over the paper's grain. That sensitive under-skin probably tingling as she smooths each wrinkle. I watch the intimacy between the caresser and the object. Then she gently pinches the corners, holds it up to the light, a single ply falls open doubling the size and halving the thickness. The white scrim blurs the contours of the window frame. She almost smiles as she spreads the napkin like a small tablecloth. Her hands meet in the center and part, meet and part, as she smooths it again then carefully lifts a two-inch overhang, taking her time to align the edge just so. She runs a single finger down the fold until the napkin fits the tray perfectly. With a jolt, I see myself in her satisfaction: I, too, enjoy being lost in the surface of things.

She stabs a strawberry and I silently cheer for the shaky bite to make it across the abyss between the container and her wide-open mouth.

My Father's Roses

Your roses went crazy last August—
blossoms echoed across the yard,
pink, yellow, and red excess.
They begged, *Where are you? Look at us.*

Last August blossoms echoed.
Too many thin shoots strangled the birdbath.
They begged, *Where are you? Look at us!*
It seemed mean that you couldn't brag.

Too many thin shoots strangled the birdbath.
Thorny tendrils unclipped and untended.
It seemed mean that you couldn't brag,
lay claim to the overabundance.

Thorny tendrils unclipped and untended,
stems drooped with weighted blooms.
You were always one for overabundance,
although your generous belly was gone.

Stems drooped with weighted blooms,
the colors were magnificent.
Although your generous belly was gone,
in your dark glasses and cotton robe,

you still bloomed, magnificent.
The roses posed giving comfort.
In your dark glasses and maroon robe,
you watched your garden loosen.

The roses posed giving comfort:
across the yard, pink, yellow, red excess.
You watched your garden loosen.
Your roses went crazy last August.

Remembering the End of Spring Street Books

The books loosened
like old teeth,
gaps widening
into book-
shaped spaces.

The Japanese
have a word for
absented places:
Yohaku no bi,
but I'll never be
Zen enough to not
project my nostalgia
into the emptiness.

The scent
of aging paper
and worn pine floors
somehow cooled
the blistering
summer heat.
The cow bell
over the door

clanged, Customer!
but the owner
rarely noticed.

I could always
pick up a free
St. Mark's Poetry Calendar
to circle happenings
and open mics
I mostly missed.

The slow neglect
to restock was killer.
The deliberate
starvation while
the guts
of the shop
were exposed—
grungy adhesive
once hidden
by inventory,
elbow-hinged shelves
designed to collapse.

The Employees Only
door left open:

just a yellow bucket
and busted equipment,
no round table
for more literary sorts.

Gone 40 years
are the local zines,
the stacks of radical
decals at the register.
Such a colorful, unprofitable
business—this looking back.

THE HOLY SPIRIT

Thank you for the coffee kindly brewed
that cold Sunday in Kingston, New York.
Nothing opened till noon.

Not a coffee shop, but a community space
and you were typing on your laptop.
I peeked in, mistaken, *Do you have coffee?*

You answered, *Yes, I have coffee*,
more in truth than invitation.
We were there to celebrate

that after 26 years of marriage,
cancer, death, autism, screwing up,
screwing up again, we sometimes still held hands.

Thank you for the coffee, a fresh pot
for our small family. Picnic-table seating,
shelves lined with used books.

My scan landed on *American Psycho*,
my daughter read *The Little Mermaid*,
my husband, unlike his reticent self, began to chat.

I read and re-read Ellis's masterful first paragraph,
imaging how I might deploy the looping structure in a poem.
You had read and loved each book for sale.

A collector also of unknown country music
with little interest in Willy, you and my husband
moved to the backroom to peruse obscure recordings,

looking for takes done in one honest shot,
bootlegs pirated by a man in an oil-cloth hat,
tape deck slung over a shoulder.

I sat reading, sipping my coffee,
my daughter echoing her Disney dialogue,
at peace in our worlds within your world.

We paid a dollar for the book, and slipped
a few bucks for the coffee into a jar.
You recommended a place called Abuela's:
When you think you've gone too far,
it's just a little farther. I thanked you
for your hospitality.

How easily you could have said no.
You had troubles of your own,
two small children at home,

and the place took all your time
from archiving and discovery.
We're in the weeds now, you sighed.

We never made it to Abuela's,
but I bought a dirty plastic ornament,
molded in the heavy resins of the 1950's—

a little girl holding a basket-of-plenty,
a dove landing on her shoulder.
I cleaned her with a cotton swab, warm water

and the colors brightened,
blossoms spilled across her pink frock,
a black shoe peeped from under the hem.

Then I noticed one of the dove's wings had broken.
The flat spot where it was sheared off
was rougher than her glossy exterior.

I wish she were mint, but she's not—
a small let-down, and then love.

THE ONCOLOGIST'S OFFICE

The sun scorched
through the bald
plate glass,

as we were forced
to sit close, share armrests.

One knit
a message
to her unborn
grandchild: *Remember Me*
in the loop and purl
of orange yarn.

One young man
was a caught deer;
wide-eyed and muscular.

Tick
the long hand
stuck,
tock
the minute
skipped.

A brew
of lemon grass
and eye-of-newt
bubbled in each of us.

We all bargained—
six goats, a gold necklace,
no smoking.

We eavesdropped
on the receptionist,
who was troubled
by a broken swing set.

Her files piled up
under a lucky horseshoe.

Have you ever made fun
of the weak?
Lied while promising?
Let an old friendship fade?

Magazine pages
turned.

We wanted to be
luxury travelers
to Belize, St. Lucia,
Tasmania, Alexandria,
the North Pole, anywhere
but The Chemo Suite
with its porous
dropped ceiling,
millions of tiny black dots.

THE BOX

The box has been delivered and set
upon the dining room table.
You read the label, shake it, and listen.
This is the visiting nurse's equipment.
Even though you know what lurks inside,
you can't help being excited by a parcel.

A few weeks ago, you prowled
the Health aisle at Barnes and Noble,
to see if *Blood in Stool* was indexed
in *The Handbook of Signs and Symptoms.*

Before all this, you were a science teacher
who liked to make collages: beads, paper,
seeds, rusted bolts, bird bones, Dali ants.
Now your butt is everyone's concern.

You no longer sit home scheming
about how to make Mendel's peas
fascinating to teens. Instead,
you spend all day focused on patterns
in dust, marble, tree bark. Everything
is such a 3-D miracle of life,
you tire of your X-ray vision.

Nurse Cherry arranges the box contents
like a Thanksgiving hostess:
biohazard disposal jug where the turkey goes,
flanked by a biohazard clean up kit,
a 9-volt battery pack as a salad plate;
some latex gloves, alcohol preps, syringes,
heparin and saline as condiments.
Instead of a hand in dinner prayer,
your balletic gesture offers a bare wrist.

She hooks you up. Amazing what one
can adjust to. The chemo should be the blue
of anti-freeze, but it's clear. Possible side effects:
nausea, vomiting, fatigue, hair loss, mouth sores,
rashes, blisters, swollen fingers and toes,
blood in urine, blood in stool, and leukemia.

You don't trust a cure that could cause leukemia,
but the side effects that bother you
aren't listed anywhere. Why do your eyes
feel smaller? Why do you smell like tin?
How have you absorbed that aroma in hospitals,
laboratories, waiting rooms?

Thank god for television—but Diane
announces Katie Couric's husband
has died of colon cancer. You begin
frantic calculations: he was 42, you are 38,
plus 4. You have GHI, he was famous,
minus 3. His was stage 4, yours stage 2,
plus 6. He had his surgery 8 months ago.

You promise to eat right, quit drinking,
quit cursing, go to church, exercise, volunteer.
You turn on America's Funniest Home Videos
because the kid with the bat will hit his dad in the nuts,
the table under the drunk dancer will collapse,
the dog on the skateboard will crash,
and it's good to know what's coming.

Cab Ride Home after Consulting with the Surgeon

-after Nazim Hikmet

In a cab on Northern Boulevard
in a light rain
the dark comes early
I never knew I loved
the brief clear
after a wiper swipe
how the drops fill it in
before the soft *thwomp*

                         clear again

I didn't know I loved
the giant necklace of red taillights
and the dramas I concoct
starring my comrades in traffic
like the woman at the stoplight
who worries about an addicted son
and the turbaned livery driver
who will soon buy a house on Long Island

And here I've loved clocks all the while
especially big public clocks

in their own personal towers
reminding me of the *luminary clock* in Frost's poem
that is both a full moon and a clock to my mind
I didn't know I loved
the Central Park clock's out-of-tune chimes
                    that messed up sweetness is just right

I didn't know I loved numbers at all
the 07124 of Santo's license
displayed on the back of his headrest
seems both lucky and permanent
or the numbers on my bathroom scale
I would miss losing and gaining
pound 158
                it's good to have weight

I didn't know I loved the weeds
I pulled in clumps then left un-bagged
in tidy piles like miniature hay bales

for pill bugs and gnats
those mysterious white specks

I didn't know I loved
these potholes and the littered field

the possibility of imagining beyond
                        the night sky

I didn't know I loved
each tiny cross in the screwheads
of the taxi door
or the muddy earth
streaked across the floormat
                I didn't know I loved

                        this ride

STRIDING FIGURE AT THE METROPOLITAN MUSEUM OF ART

The moment I spy you
in Mesopotamian Art,
I begin to Tootsie Roll.
5,000 years old,
and you got it all going on—
Nobody struts like you strut
in that horned Sunday hat
and raptor cloak, fists up
as your arms pump
while you take a firm step
in those enviable boots.
Glory to your maker!
Take my hand and shuffle me
through this hallowed gallery.
Let's two-hop the grand stairs.
Tonight, free swing
at Lincoln Center.
Cock your hat
and twirl me,
sashay me,
deep dip me, please.
My flouncy dress
bounces in time

as we quickstep
across the floor.
The band strikes up
Ain't She Sweet
and you cut-a-rug
in your patina boots.
Toss your raptor
cloak across a café chair.
Your bronze skin shines
with sweat so when
you pull me in for a kiss
my hands slip
most deliciously
down your smooth,
sculpted chest.
Let's stay drunk
while we spin.
So there's a 4,950 year
age difference,
I like your style,
your confidence.
Escort me forever,
dance me away
from the cases
of broken pottery
and lost medallions

to a place where
we can jig
through millennia,
swagger among
monsoons,
moonwalk
while empires
crumble.

ACKNOWLEDGMENTS

Grateful acknowledgment is made to the editors of the journals and anthologies who first published the following poems.

Midwest Review: "Directions"

Ampersand: "When"; "Striding Figure at the Metropolitan"

Chicago Quarterly Review: "Dear Pluto"; "The Scholar's Courtyard at the Metropolitan Museum of Art"

Gravity Pulls You In: "How to Talk to an Autistic Child"

Brain, Child: "We Count to Three" (online)

Alaska Quarterly Review: "Etymology"; "Telescope Stilts"

New Ohio Review: "Why It's Hard to Write About My Brother"; "She-Monster Gets Fired"

Epiphany: The Writers Studio at 30: "She-Monster Gets Fired"

Patterson Literary Review: "The Box"

Gemini: "Powerful Forces" (online)

Salamander: "To My Old Lewis Turco *The Book of Forms"* ;"The Old Cat"

Rhino: "The Oncologist's Office"

Pirene's Fountain: To Jon Anderson (Online)

Earlier versions of the following poems appeared in my chapbook, *The Familiar,* published by Finishing Line Press in 2011: "To Jon Anderson"; "The Scholar's Courtyard at the Metropolitan Museum of Art"; "Our Father's Roses"; "How to Talk to an Autistic Child"; "We Count to three"; "When"; "The Box" and "Red Graffiti".

"Dear Pluto"; "The Oncologist's Office"; "Striding Figure"; "Etymology"; "Ode to a Dumpster"; "Cab Ride Home after Consulting with the Surgeon" and "To My Old Lewis Turco *The Book of Forms*" appeared, often in earlier versions, in a second chapbook, *The Brief Clear,* published by Finishing Line Press, 2015.

NOTES

"Ode to the Turtle" is indebted to "Ode to the Chameleon" by Yusef Komunyakaa.

"The Oncologist's Office" is indebted to Dorothy Barresi's poem "Security" from *American Fanatics.*

"Walking to LaGuardia Community College" is indebted to Ross Gay's poem "to the fig tree on 9th and christian" from *catalog of unabashed gratitude.*

"Meditation on George the Snail" was inspired by Julia Jacobs' article "George the Snail, Believed to Be the Last of His Species, Dies at 14 in Hawaii" in *The New York Times*, January 10, 2019.

Epigraph: Ted Kooser, excerpt from "Mother" from Delights & Shadows. Copyright © 2004 by Ted Kooser. Reprinted with the permission of The Permissions Company, LLC on behalf of Copper Canyon Press, coppercanyonpress.org.

Image Titles in Order of Appearance

Dinosaurs to Birds; Rob Thinking; Baggage; Duplicate/No Duplicate; Powerful Forces; Befuddled; Lone Fox; Driven by Feeling (published by Apricity Press, 2023); Dream Door; Playground; The Brass Tag; Mother; She Told Me It Looked Like Africa

ABOUT THE AUTHOR

Kim Farrar is a writer and collage artist. Her full-length poetry collection, *The Impossible Physics of the Hummingbird*, is forthcoming from Unsolicited Press in 2025. She is the author of two chapbooks, *The Familiar* and *The Brief Clear*, both published by Finishing Line Press. Her poetry has appeared in *Alaska Quarterly Review*, *Chicago Quarterly Review*, *Salamander*, *Rhino*, *New Ohio Review* and other literary journals. Her essays have been published in *Illness & Grace, Voices of Autism,* and *Reflections.* Her manuscripts, *The Impossible Physics of the Hummingbird* and *Calamities of the Natural World*, were semi-finalists in Grayson's poetry contests in 2022 and 2021 respectively. *Orbits and Bonds,* a chapbook of poems and collages, was a semi-finalist in the New Women's Voices contest by Finishing Line Press in 2022. In 2020 her poem "Powerful Forces" received an honorable mention in the *Gemini* Poetry Contest. She is a three-time Pushcart Prize nominee.

ABOUT THE PRESS

Unsolicited Press is based out of Portland, Oregon and focuses on the works of the unsung and underrepresented. As a womxn-owned, all-volunteer small publisher that doesn't worry about profits as much as championing exceptional literature, we have the privilege of partnering with authors skirting the fringes of the lit world. We've worked with emerging and award-winning authors such as Amy Shimshon-Santo, Brook Bhagat, Elisa Carlsen, Tara Stillions Whitehead, and Anne Leigh Parrish.

Learn more at unsolicitedpress.com. Find us on Instagram, X, Facebook, Pinterest, Bsky, Threads, YouTube, and LinkedIn. Unsolicited Press also writes a snarky newsletter on Substack.